# Your EPIC Experiment!

### A 90-Day Personal Challenge 1.0

Sue Hiser

Copyright © 2018 Sue Hiser.

All rights reserved. No part of this book may be reproduced, stored, or transmitted by any means—whether auditory, graphic, mechanical, or electronic—without written permission of the author, except in the case of brief excerpts used in critical articles and reviews. Unauthorized reproduction of any part of this work is illegal and is punishable by law.

This book is a work of non-fiction. Unless otherwise noted, the author and the publisher make no explicit guarantees as to the accuracy of the information contained in this book and in some cases, names of people and places have been altered to protect their privacy.

ISBN: 978-1-4834-7971-2 (sc)
ISBN: 978-1-4834-7972-9 (e)

Because of the dynamic nature of the Internet, any web addresses or links contained in this book may have changed since publication and may no longer be valid. The views expressed in this work are solely those of the author and do not necessarily reflect the views of the publisher, and the publisher hereby disclaims any responsibility for them.

Any people depicted in stock imagery provided by Thinkstock are models, and such images are being used for illustrative purposes only.
Certain stock imagery © Thinkstock.

Lulu Publishing Services rev. date: 1/18/2018

# AUTHOR'S NOTE

*This book is not perfect, none of us are, but despite that lack of perfection you hold 1.0 in your hands. I've focused on this journal being 1.0 and am open to continuing to evolve it via other avenues and into the next version.*

*Here's what I believe . . . there's someone out there who needs this journal and it could be you. Actually, just assume it is you. You are the one who is to go down this path and make this journey to achieve your goal. This journal is one of the tools along your journey. Together we are destined to make your dream and epic journey come alive. I am doing this for people who I don't even know, but I know are looking for a helping hand.*

And here's a great quote to get us started:

> **"Do not wait; the time will never be 'just right.' Start where you stand, and work with whatever tools you may have at your command, and better tools will be found as you go along."** —*George Herbert*

Begin by reading and signing the following:

I_____(fill in your name) commit to beginning a 90-day personal challenge. My journey will have challenges, but I am open to discovery and experimentation.

Signed: _____

Date: _____

And, here's space for your quote:

# INTRODUCTION

Epic!! Why is this an Epic experiment? Because this is yours, and no one else's. These 90-days are yours to do with as you wish and the chance to challenge yourself in new and exciting ways or even to tackle an old goal in a new way.

We live in VUCA times - Volatile, Uncertain, Complex and Ambiguous. You feel it in all aspects of your life and maybe you've been trying to control the ride. But, maybe a different approach is needed. Maybe you should give into the ride and try new approaches, new mindsets, learn from others, share your successes and your failures in the process and keep on going.

Why 90-days? We like immediate gratification and while 90-days doesn't feel long in some ways, especially to do something epic, it's long enough to see change, create momentum and be a catalyst for your longer term goals and for someone else's goals. That's right. You might be a catalyst for someone else's goals and dreams. Your actions to dive into your epic journey and experiment may be all about being the motivator for someone else.

This book is a mini guide to the process and the journal that will document your success. Oh, you will be successful. If you record your goals, experiment with new approaches, record what you learn, you will be successful. Will it be the success you wanted from the beginning? Well it may be or it may be something even more exciting! Your goal is to immerse yourself in the process and add some youthful exuberance. You haven't felt youthful for a while? That's okay. Go to a playground and watch the little ones play and you'll see the exuberance you've been lacking that has been sitting dormant in you and waiting to come out and engage. Don't like kids? Check out puppies on Youtube and start to laugh again.

What else should we add? How about adding experimentation and learning? This is not a pass/fail course. Everything that happens is part of your experiment and an aspect of learning for you. Turn off the judgement voice and turn on the 'Hmmm – I didn't know that." This is the voice of the observer who sees things anew and looks for new meaning and understanding.

90-Days! Here we go!

# PRINCIPLES OF AN EPIC EXPERIMENT

What is an EPIC experiment? Well it can be anything you want it to be, and you'll explore that soon. I've added principles to give you some further insights as to what the EPIC experiment can be and the impact. Principles according to the google dictionary are: " . . .a fundamental truth or proposition that serves as the foundation for a system of belief or behavior or for a chain of reasoning."

Principle 1: An EPIC experiment builds a better you.

Principle 2: An EPIC experiment taps into potential and possibility in a way you never have before.

Principle 3: An EPIC experiment addresses and removes one or more barriers.

Principle 4: An EPIC experiment fills a need for you and for others.

Principle 5: An EPIC experiment is a choice that gives energy.

Principle 6: An EPIC experiment inspires yourself and inspires others through your actions.

Principle 7: An EPIC experiment is about creating a new reality.

Principle 8: An EPIC experiment challenges you to connect with your true self.

Principle 9: An EPIC experiment allows you to learn at a deeper level.

Principle 10: An EPIC experiment helps you know you are NOT alone. There are others who support you either directly or indirectly, and you are part of something much bigger.

Principle 11: (you fill this one in)_____

Principle 12: (you fill this one in)_____

# GETTING STARTED!

I'll tell you more about the genesis of this experiment in Appendix B, but for now let's get you started. What do you want to tackle in the next 90-Days? There are six 'explorations' for you to explore what you want to do. Write down your initial thoughts below for **Exploration #1:**

If you need a few ideas here are a few approaches for **Exploration #2**.

Many people think in terms of New Year's resolutions and that's okay to start the process. Here are the top New Year's resolutions:

- Exercise more (38 per cent)
- Lose weight (33 per cent)
- Eat more healthily (32 per cent)
- Take a more active approach to health (15 per cent)
- Learn new skill or hobby (15 per cent)
- Spend more time on personal wellbeing (12 per cent)
- Spend more time with family and friends (12 per cent)
- Drink less alcohol (12 per cent)
- Stop smoking (9 per cent)
- Other (1 per cent)

Source: ComRes poll (http://www.telegraph.co.uk/health-fitness/body/common-new-years-resolutions-stick/)

Are those epic? Do you kind of sigh when you read that list because there is no surprise there for you? I understand completely. You need to go for something that excites you, something that will wake you up on a rainy Monday morning because you can't wait to tackle it. Record what strikes you from the above list but take it to another level. For example: I want to exercise more so I can do an Ironman Triathlon (THAT is an EPIC challenge)! Another example: I want to create a journal that others will use for their EPIC experiment.

So look at the initial list and then take it to the next level if something catches your attention!

**Exploration #3:** Has someone said something recently or have you seen something in the media that has made you stop and think? Maybe that's another clue. Record what is catching your attention. . .

I have a friend who was turning 50 and a college friend wanted to celebrate this milestone with her by doing something EPIC. She called her months before and announced, "We are backpackers!" The 49-year old said, "No, we're not." But before she knew it she was climbing stairs in preparation for a trip and an experience of a lifetime. The lesson here is to think of the friend you can drag with you into an EPIC experiment.
**What friend do you want to join you?**_____

**Why this person?**_____
This could be another clue for your EPIC challenge and a support person to tap into during your experiment.

**What are the attributes you like about this person (and don't stop at just one or two – keep going to the end of this page)?**

**Let's continue the Exploration #4.** Here's another approach. What don't you like in your life right now? What are the negatives? Make that list and then imagine that the reverse is true and write them as positives. I've read about this approach from a few different sources but a sweet book, especially if you've ever wanted to write a book, about someone who references this approach is Susan Branch in her book, 'Martha Vineyard Isle of Dreams'. Check out page 181 for her list, but here's a sample after she switched her negatives to positives:

"I choose to give myself one gold star a week.
I choose to eat healthy.
I choose to write a cookbook."

| Record a few ideas for yourself (I've given you room for 10 but continue to explore): ||
|---|---|
| What I don't like in my life right now... | What I want it to be... |
| | |
| | |
| | |
| | |
| | |
| | |
| | |
| | |
| | |
| | |

**Let's continue with Exploration #5.**

Category Approach: This is also a classic approach and can follow along with the negative to positive. This time you think in terms of categories (I use the acronym ESPM):

Emotional needs:




Spiritual needs:




Physical needs:




Mental needs:

Let's continue with **Exploration #6.**

Desire approach: This was a unique one from Danielle Laport, 'The Desire Map: A Guide to Creating Goals with Soul'. She makes a great point that our goals are about desires or the feelings attached to the goals. You'll ask yourself different questions in this approach and one thing that intrigued me was her comment that you can't desire self-confidence. Self-confidence is a by-product to success and not the end result. I've mentioned this comment to a number of people in presentations and it always strikes a chord with attendees.

> **"Motivation is not a thinking word;
> it's a feeling word." – John Kotter**

The initial questions are simple: How do I want to feel? And what do I need to do to feel that way? Make a few notes here to those two questions:

All of these are part of the exploration to get to the point where you find the right thing that speaks to you and makes you say, "YES – that's where I want to focus my time and energy for the next 90 days!" Make a few notes of what you've discovered so far and use pictures, words etc. to note your epiphanies. Have a lot of ideas? Focus and choose 1 for your EPIC Experiement.

WATER: When all else fails in coming up with ideas – take a shower!

When I ask groups of people when and where they come up with their best ideas the typical responses include: running, walking the dog, driving to work, playing with the kids, taking a shower. I've also heard of writers who just take showers when they need ideas and hit a road block. Notice the response is never sitting at the desk or in the office. Rarely does an epiphany come when you are in a meeting either.

Now is a good time to walk away and go into nature before you tackle the next piece. Go for a walk, take the dog, grab the kids or just take a shower. Let everything you have gathered to this point incubate, have it run through a few filters in your mind and let the processing occur while you engage in something else.

Don't worry – everything will be right here waiting for you.

**Welcome back! Draft:** Isn't it funny how saying 'draft' relaxes you a little and allows the pen to stand ready for work versus frozen that this has to be THE answer. Nothing in this book is THE answer. All of the things you record are part of your experiment that allows you to shape the answers, the outcomes, the learnings. You are the meaning maker – your job is to keep the meaning positive and moving forward.

DRAFT

My EPIC experiment is: _____

I commit to the following in the next 90 days:
_____
_____
_____
_____

I am:_____

(Name and claim your goal and become that person!)

Why this experiment is important to me:

Reason 1 _____

Reason 2 _____

Reason 3_____

Reason 4_____

Reason 5_____

I will know I'm successful when: _____
_____

Answer the following questions about your initial draft. . . .

What I really like about my draft:

What I would really like to change about my draft:

The feelings and desires I am looking for in this challenge are!

The following would make my draft awesome!

# FIRST VERSION

Now that you've had the chance to reflect on your first draft make some adjustments to create your first version. First version is another draft with a little refinement, but still this is not in stone. And, we may never be in stone. This is about building momentum. Everything is about building momentum and seeing what works.

Version One

My EPIC experiment is: _____

I commit to the following in the next 90 days:
_____
_____
_____
_____

I am: _____
(Name and claim your goal and become that person – now!)

Why this challenge important to me:

**Reason 1**


**Reason 2**


**Reason 3**

**Reason 4**


**Reason 5**


I will know I'm successful when:
_____

**"If you can dream it, you can do it." —Walt Disney**

(How can you argue with Mickey's Dad?)

**Overview**: Your 90-Day Epic Experiment covers approximately 3 months, or 12 weeks. The objective is to break the larger goal into smaller doable goals that you can tackle on a weekly basis. As you experiment with each week you learn, have success, learn some more, take more risks, and continually build momentum. Along the way you'll have celebrations, learn from others and make modifications. Infuse as much fun into the process as you can otherwise it just seems like another task on a list, and I doubt if that's what you need. I anticipate you want success, something new, not a to-do.

Journals need to be fun and engaging. A journal for an EPIC Experiment should tell a story, your story! Periodically you'll see some fun things to take notes in a different way, maybe meet someone you really love (and hopefully that would be to yourself), check out a youtube video, experience something new. I want you to look back on this journal in five or ten years and be inspired by what you did. Or, imagine a younger person picking it up in a few years and being in awe that **this** is what got you into gear for all of the exciting things you are doing now! What would make it eye catching? Consider doing the following:

- Tape in pictures, quotes, articles
- Use different color ink
- Add stickers (Be a kid again)
- Let someone else add a note of encouragement

Here's a guideline for you to follow as you use the journal. The pages are laid out for weekly goals and reflections, daily notes, and monthly celebrations. There is less recording in one week than another. Variety is provided so you can explore what works for you. Make changes as you see fit. Somedays you'll want more. Other days you'll want less. Use what's there and explore. Be mindful of when the critical voice jumps in and tells you to stop because something isn't right. This is the voice that might have stopped you in the past. NOT THIS TIME!

Thank the critical voice for their input, but inform them you are venturing forward for 12 weeks with or without them. If the voice continues chatting imagine giving them a baby pacifier and imagine putting whatever taste you want on that baby pacifier to satisfy, quiet and soothe that critical voice. Your critical voice is trying to save you from failure. There is no failure, there are only things to try and learn from. Note: I told the pacifier trick to a group once and the next time we met their executive handed out little pacifiers to each leader. Whatever works, works! Buy a pacifier if your critic needs it.

Once you have your EPIC experiment created you'll revisit it each week to determine the progress you've made and the steps you want to take in the next week.

Each week:

1. Revisit your overall goal
2. Record feedback on your progress for that week and to date
3. Establish a new sub goal for the next week

**Fun Activity: Redecorate the cover of this journal.** This is a slim book for a reason. I want you to have it with you to make notes and I want it to speak to you. Decorate the cover with pictures, quotes, phrases, etc.- anything that connects with your challenge and will make you stop and think. Brainstorm ideas and record in the space below by looking at the pictures on your phone, and looking at your music playlist. And, guess what? You can change your cover at any time in the process. Take a picture of the old and create the new one over the old.

**Re-creation is all part of EPIC challenges.**

**My 90 Day EPIC Experiment is:**
_____

**In the first 30 days I want to:**
_____

### WEEK ONE:

My challenge is:

My goal for this week is to:

My biggest obstacle is:

My strategy to overcome this obstacle is:

**WAIT! Check the continuum below - after recording the goals for Week One do you feel more panic, or more courage?**

Panic  _____Panic (Tipping Point to . . .)_____Courageous

Notice these two words exist on a continuum, and maybe you vacillate from one point to another. Either response creates an easier week than you are expecting because you are to focus on 'noticing' this week. **Tackle whatever element of your goal you feel comfortable taking on, but the main thing is to notice and really see what is going on around you, and inside you.** Remember this is an EPIC experiment so you need to don an experimenter's hat or coat, or their persona. Otherwise the pull of old behaviors, mindsets, memories will drag you back to struggle and to potentially stop all together. And, if or when you share your EPIC experiment with someone their inner critic could jump out at YOU! I know – what the heck! The things we do **to** friends. Experimenting makes people pause and think of just trying something, for example another kind of ice-cream. How innocent is that? Your job this week is to notice and see what's going on. And, let's take noticing one step further by giving yourself some feedback. Check out the rating scale below and you'll have pages to record your rating and observations.

**Rate yourself!** Come up with a way to score yourself on your success each day. This is feedback, and you need feedback to build confidence in yourself. Here are a few options:

1. Yes/no – At the end of the day did you do what you wanted to do? Did you take time to notice what was going on around you? Yes or no. This is a good rating, but can be tough for perfectionists and can lead to defeatist thinking unless you realize 'noticing' that you did not do something is better than never having the 'intention' in the first place.
2. 1/2/3 Scale- This is a tweak on yes/no. 1 equals 'no', 2 equals 'meets', and 3 is 'exceeds'. For the math wizard in you, this process allows you to get something for good intentions because recognizing that you did not do what you wanted to do and receiving a point is still some level of gratification. Plus, the recording of the process brings you closer to your real intention. Recording numbers versus a series of 'no's' will eventually make you realize that something has to change!
3. 1 – 3 stars: Using the same scale above you give yourself stars on what you've done.

**The potential 'notice' responses could include:**

Rating: Yes – I noticed things about my situation that I did not notice before including. . .

Rating: 2 I rated myself a 2 on noticing because there were some I saw immediately, but others I didn't notice until now

Rating: * I give myself one star for just recording this in my EPIC journal tonight

**For your first week you have a half-page to record your observations AND if you just want to take a picture of what you notice with your phone – do that! A picture is worth a 1000 words and easier to do for many people. Then just make a note of what the picture was.**

**Guess what? There are no wrong answers. You are the meaning maker – whatever happens is just data for your experiment. And wait until you see the great quote at the end of week one! It's a great reframing.**

## WEEK 1 – DAY 1: FEEDBACK AND REPORTING

Begin by scoring yourself and then answer the following questions:

Rating: _____

1. **Notice**: What was your biggest discovery today in relation to your goal to notice?
2. What insight does your discovery give you?
3. What do you want to look for tomorrow?

## DAY 2: FEEDBACK AND REPORTING – SAME QUESTIONS AS ABOVE

Rating: _____

## WEEK 1 DAY 3: FEEDBACK AND REPORTING (NEW QUESTION)

Rating: _____

1. **Notice**: What was your biggest discovery today in relation to your goal to notice?
2. What insight does your discovery give you?
3. Where do you see momentum for your experiment?

## DAY 4: FEEDBACK AND REPORTING – SAME QUESTIONS AS ABOVE

Rating: _____

# WEEK 1 – DAY 5: FEEDBACK AND REPORTING

Rating: _____

1. **Notice**: What was your biggest discovery today in relation to your goal to notice?
2. What insight does your discovery give you?
3. What excites you for tomorrow?

# DAY 6: FEEDBACK AND REPORTING – SAME QUESTIONS AS ABOVE

Rating: _____

# WEEK 1 DAY 7: FEEDBACK AND REPORTING

Rating: _____

1. **Notice**: What was your biggest discovery today in relation to your goal to notice?
2. What insight does your discovery give you?
3. What is your plan for tomorrow?

**YOU DID IT! YOU FINISHED WEEK ONE! YOU NEED TO CELEBRATE! WHAT WILL YOU DO TO CELELBRATE?**

**Great quote (as promised): "The devil whispered in my ear, "You're not strong enough to withstand the storm." Today I whispered in the devil's ear, "I am the storm."**

**How's that for an EPIC quote for an EPIC experimenter?! Be the storm!**

# WEEK 1 SUMMARY & WEEK 2 LAUNCH!

What excited me most about this week was:

What I learned about myself this week was:

**90 Day EPIC Challenge:**

---

**In the first 30 days I want to:**

---

> "Believe in yourself! Have faith in your abilities! Without a humble but reasonable confidence in your own powers you cannot be successful or happy." —Norman Vincent Peale

## WEEK TWO:

My challenge is:

My goal for this week is to:

My biggest obstacle is:

My strategy to overcome this obstacle is:

**Activity: Why you and why now?!:** Isn't it interesting when people share their accomplishments and tell you their story, it all makes sense. Everything they've ever done has prepared them for that exact moment to reach the goal, overcome the obstacle and to stand on their internal stage and be proud. There isn't always external acclaim. It's their inner feeling of accomplishment that shines through and provides the exclamation point to the story. So, let's play with that and create that story. When you tell the story of your EPIC accomplishment imagine sharing the following:

1. Why you were motivated to do what you did.
2. The unique life experiences that prepared you for this journey.
3. The abilities you have that made you the expert or the success.
4. What your super power was or the special sauce that brought it all together that made this unique and successful for you.

Imagine sitting around a campfire or at a bar and share your incredible story of success. Make a few notes and use the next page to record your EPIC story.

# WEEK 2 DAY 1: FEEDBACK AND REPORTING

Rating: _____

1. What was your biggest success today in relation to your goal?
2. How is today's experiences part of your EPIC story you created? If it's not there – should something be added to your EPIC story?

Remember: You overcoming obstacles helps others believe they can too!

## WEEK 2 DAY 2: FEEDBACK AND REPORTING

Rating: _____

1. What was your biggest success today in relation to your goal?
2. How is today's experiences part of your EPIC story you created? If it's not there – should something be added to your EPIC story?

# WEEK 2 DAY 3: FEEDBACK AND REPORTING

Rating: _____

1. What was your biggest success today in relation to your goal?
2. What chapter headings are coming to mind for your EPIC experiment story?

# WEEK 2 DAY 4: FEEDBACK AND REPORTING

Rating: _____

1. What was your biggest success today in relation to your goal?
2. What chapter headings are coming to mind for your EPIC experiment story?

# WEEK 2 DAY 5: FEEDBACK AND REPORTING

Rating: _____

1. What was your biggest success today in relation to your goal?
2. How is today's experiences part of your EPIC story you created? If it's not there – should something be added to your EPIC story?

## WEEK 2 DAY 6: FEEDBACK AND REPORTING

Rating: _____

1. What was your biggest success today in relation to your goal?
2. How is today's experiences part of your EPIC story you created? If it's not there – should something be added to your EPIC story?

## DAY 7: FEEDBACK AND REPORTING – SAME QUESTIONS AS ABOVE

**WEEK 2 SUMMARY:** Impressive how you are still working on your goal. You know some people have stopped, but not you. Second week isn't easy to keep momentum moving. What little things happened that show you are on the right path? Record what you've seen, heard, experienced, and felt.

Remember 'the universe favors the brave' (need to find out who said THAT). CONTINUE TO BE BRAVE! And BE COURAGEOUS!

What excited me most about week 2 was:

What I learned about myself in week 2 was:

## WEEK 3 LAUNCH!

**90 Day EPIC Challenge:**

---

**In the first 30 days I want to:**

---

### WEEK THREE:

My challenge is:

My goal for this week is to:

My biggest obstacle is:

My strategy to overcome this obstacle is:

**It's time for a change! You need new approaches, new monitoring, new ways to capture your thoughts. Week 3 is only two pages – make notes using the categories, but also create your own. There's two extra pages just for you to reflect and have some insights, or pictures, or . . . whatever makes you happy.**

**I'm around amazing people and so are you. Here are a couple of ideas people have used to signal to themselves on a daily basis that they are in the midst of an EPIC experiment and want to make some level of change.**

- One woman who wanted to work on a new leadership behavior went to her hair stylist and changed her hair style. Every time she looked in the mirror she was reminded she was trying something new.
- Purchase and wear a new watch. One man said it signaled to him that it was 'a new time' and to be open to new ideas.
- Move the trash receptacle in your office. Excellent idea if you are trying to change an unconscious habit. This illustrates how your environment influences you every day. (Not recommended to do in the kitchen).

You also have extra columns to create your own 'thing' to track. And, two extra pages to make whatever notes you need.

| Week 3: One pager | Describe the perfect day in relation to your EPIC Challenge | What really happened? | What surprised you in a positive way? |
|---|---|---|---|
| Day 1 | | | |
| Day 2 | | | |
| Day 3 | | | |
| Day 4 | | | |
| Day 5 | | | |
| Day 6 | | | |
| Day 7 | | | |

|  | Additional Notes: create your own categories (BTW – HAVE FUN WITH THIS!) | | |
|---|---|---|---|
|  |  |  |  |
| Day 1 |  |  |  |
| Day 2 |  |  |  |
| Day 3 |  |  |  |
| Day 4 |  |  |  |
| Day 5 |  |  |  |
| Day 6 |  |  |  |
| Day 7 |  |  |  |

WEEK 3: YOUR EXTRA PAGE 1 OF 2

# WEEK 3: YOUR EXTRA PAGE 2 OF 2

**WEEK 3 SUMMARY:** Have someone pretend to be your coach and have them ask you the following questions. They can either write the notes or you can do so, or tape the conversation.

## COACH QUESTIONS:

1. What was your biggest accomplishment in the past week?

2. How will you celebrate your accomplishment?

3. What is ONE thing from last week that you want to take into your next week?

4. How important is your EPIC goal to you REALLY?

5. Rate your performance this week on a scale of 1- 10, 10 being the best. What would you do this week that would raise your score one notch higher?

6. What is one thing you want to do different this next week?

# WEEK 4 LAUNCH!

Week 4 and sometimes EPIC work can feel forced. This week is about going to a different realm besides 'force'. Instead I want you to explore 'power'. The reference for this is the book by David Hawkins 'Power versus Force: The Hidden Determinants of Human Behavior'. The list below illustrates contrasting patterns between a higher energy pattern (words on the left) and a lower energy pattern (words on the right). As you review the list, consider how you use either one of the elements in your EPIC experiment now. When you are using more of the elements on the left, are you seeing more momentum? Do you see how the ones on the right, have not created the same type of momentum? Review the list and determine how to integrate more power into your daily actions. See the box below for a sample.

Abundant....Excessive
Accepting....Rejecting
Admitting....Denying
Allowing....Controlling
Approving....Critical
Balanced...Extreme
Being....Having
Believing...Insisting
Brilliant...Clever
Challenged...Impeded
**Choosing-to...Having – to** ⟶
Concerned....Judgmental
Confident...Arrogant
Conscious...Unaware
Courageous...Reckless
Detached..Removed
Determined...Stubborn
Devoted...Possessive
Doing...Getting
Educating...Persuading
Encouraging...Promoting

> As you establish your plan for this week and identify the behaviors and the tasks that will move you closer to your goal, keep in mind that you are 'choosing-to' do these things, not 'having-to'. Choice is power, having to do something is being forced. Words matter – choose the ones that give you power!

Energetic... Agitated
Envisioning...Picturing
Essential... Apparent
Excellent... Adequate
Experienced... Cynical
Flexible... Rigid
Forgiving... Resenting
Gifted... Lucky
Grateful... Indebted
Holistic... Analytic
Inspired... Mundane
Inventive...Prosaic
Liberating...Restricting
Long-term... Immediate
Observant...Suspicious
Optimisitic... Pessimistic
Powerful.. Forceful
Praising...Flattering
**\*Purposeful... Desirous**
Requesting... Demanding
Serene...Dull
Serving... Ambitious
**\*Significant... Important**
Spontaneous... Impulsive
Spiritual... Materialist
Striving...Struggling
Surrendering...Worrying
Tolerant... Faddish
Trusting...Gullible
Unselfish...Selfish

**Combine two**: Your EPIC challenge is important and desirous to you, but notice what is paired with those two words. How can your EPIC experiment be 'significant and purposeful'?

DON'T' YOU LOVE WORDS? They are so innocent and yet, so important and profound. Use wisely.

Note: Do you see how we used observant in week one versus suspicious? Your inner critic is suspicious; your true self is observant and doesn't judge. Hmmmmm....

Note: This is not the complete list, check page 120 – 121 of David Hawkins book "Power Versus Force' to have the complete list.

Let's play with this concept this week for our Week 4 monitoring!

## WEEK 4 LAUNCH

In the first 30 days I want to: _____

This week I choose to: _____

## POWER VS FORCE

| Week 4 | Graph your power versus force for each day! | |
|---|---|---|
| Review the list of words and using them as your reference, place a dot where you were the majority of the day and identify the words that described the day. | | What surprised you in a positive way? |
| Day 1 | POWER | FORCE |
| Day 2 | POWER | FORCE |
| Day 3 | POWER | FORCE |
| Day 4 | POWER | FORCE |
| Day 5 | POWER | FORCE |
| Day 6 | POWER | FORCE |
| Day 7 | POWER | FORCE |

# WEEK 4 POWER VS. FORCE (EXTRA PAGES)

# WEEK 4 REFLECT AND CELEBRATE!

**90 Day EPIC Challenge:** _____

**In the first 30 days I achieved!**
_____

Coach yourself this week – and begin by congratulating yourself. You've made it through the first 30 days!

1. How did you use your power vs. force? What was the impact?

2. What was your 30 day goal? How did you do?

3. What have you learned about yourself in the first 30 days?

4. What was your biggest success?

**CELEBRATE!!!! How will you celebrate your first 30 days?**

**DID YOU REALLY CELEBRATE OR ARE YOU JUST GOING ONTO THE NEXT PAGE?** You've really accomplished something by being here – 30 days in and you are still in your EPIC Experiment. You realize you are conscious of what you are doing. You are courageous, determined and really doing this! You are focused on long-term (60 more days to go). You are optimistic, purposeful, striving and trusting – yourself. Yes, all of these are power words and each describes you. If you think 'Awesome – that's me.' Go onto the next week.

**Hmmmm – if you scoff at this little paragraph and say 'not me', but secretly you wish it were you. Well, venture on EPIC wanna-be, possibilities always await the ones willing to turn the page.**

# WEEK 5 LAUNCH:

**SOMETHING NEW (Well, you've probably been using these already, but let's increase intentionality!):**

**List your 5 signature character strengths:**

1.

2.

3.

4.

5.

**How do you know your signature character strengths? Here's a few ideas:**

1. Maybe you've done a few assessments and you can pull from those resources including:
   a. FREE RESOURCE: www.viacharacter.org/survey (Complete it in less than 15 minutes)
   b. Purchase book: Strengthsfinder 2.0
2. Ask yourself the following questions:
   a. What excites me?
   b. What am I doing when I lose track of time?
   c. What am I doing when I stand out from others?
3. Ask people who know you and support you the following questions:
   a. What do I do well that you wish you could do?
   b. What do you see me doing when I'm excited?
   c. What am I doing when I stand out from others?

Why is it important to know your strengths? According to Jane McGonigal in 'SuperBetter', "... signature strengths speak to your deepest values, to what you cherish most, to what brings meaning and purpose to your life." (p. 270)

WOW! That sounds like a great add to your EPIC challenge!

### WEEK FIVE:

My challenge is:

My strengths are:

My goal for this week is to use my strengths to achieve my goal!

The area I see my biggest opportunity to use my strengths is:

I will use my strength(s) in the following way:

**Example:** Strength is Love of learning

Application: Explore different approaches others have used to achieve your goal. What do the experts say?

| WEEK 5 | My Five Strengths:<br>1.<br>2.<br>3.<br>4.<br>5. | | |
|---|---|---|---|
| **How I plan to use my strengths! Note: you could use a combination of your strengths** | **What really happened?** | **What surprised you in a positive way?** | |
| Day 1 | | | |
| Day 2 | | | |
| Day 3 | | | |
| Day 4 | | | |
| Day 5 | | | |
| Day 6 | | | |
| Day 7 | | | |

WEEK 5 EXTRA PAGES:

**Week 5 Summary:** Coach yourself this week – and begin by congratulating yourself.

1. What strength fueled your success?

2. What strength do you think you're not using? Which one do you feel most drawn to?

3. If you combined the element that caused your biggest success with what you feel drawn to – what could you create that you can take into the next 30 days?

**Week Six LAUNCH – Impressive – you've made it through 5 weeks and have used 5 different approaches for discovery, monitoring and experimenting. You've used:**

1. Noticing – This was about observing all that is occurring around you to help you in your quest.
2. Story-telling – You've created your story of success and seen how pieces are coming alive on a daily basis
3. Perfect day – You've imagined your perfect day to set expectation which drives the story to a day-to-day event.
4. Power vs. Force – You've explored the use of energetic words and intentions to maximize behaviors.
5. Strengths – You've tapped into your own strengths to see how you can use your best personal resources

**Week Six** is for you to explore using a mix of the approaches you've played with as well as adding approaches that have worked for you in the past, or ideas you want to explore. This is not freewheeling. This week is still intentional but experiential. You are building on what you've learned to date. Answer these questions and then create your approach and intention:

1. In the past 5 weeks I have learned 3 key things:



2. The easiest approach for me of the 5 was:



3. Choose either an approach that has worked for you in the past or something you've always wanted to explore.

4. Imagine: Close your eyes and imagine the answers to the above questions are written on cards that are on a table before you. Or, go ahead and write them on cards and place them on the table. How do you see them combining to create a unique approach for you this week?

5. My primary intention for this week is listed below and joins with my new approach for this week to create the following:

6. My tracking for this week will be:

I'm providing you four blank pages for this week as well as a summary page to debrief your success. Blank pages can be daunting, so you'll see the following on each page: Explore, *Try,* **Create**, LEARN and *Try again.*

Explore, *Try*, **Create**, LEARN and ***Try again.***

Explore, *Try*, **Create**, LEARN and *<u>Try again.</u>*

Explore, *Try*, **Create**, LEARN and ***Try again.***

Explore, *Try*, **Create**, LEARN and *<u>Try again.</u>*

**Week 6 Summary & Congratulations!** You, my friend, are an EPIC warrior, not just an EPIC experimenter. This past week was not easy and you took on the challenge – even if you did worst case scenario and recorded nothing, but turned to this page – it's still good because you just learned something about yourself. Didn't you? And, be nice to yourself. If your struggle to say something positive imagine you are talking to your best friend. Help them see what is positive about your current state.

What I learned about myself this week was:

What excited me most about this week was:

I am most proud about myself because I:

# WEEK 7 LAUNCH!

Let's start with a quote: " Don't let the noise of others' opinions drown out your own inner voice. And most important, have the courage to follow your heart and intuition. They somehow already know what you truly want to become. Everything else is secondary." Steve Jobs

You have a variety of voices chatting to you on a daily basis. Unfortunately they are not all positive. Periodically you might have the voice of judgement, doubt, guilt criticism (who we've already given a pacifier) and fear driving your thought process and you could mistake them for the real you. In coaching we learn that the coachee has the answers. Our role is to help them discover the answer through questions, patience and helping them see where there is possibility.

This week you try a different approach and you have the chance to work virtually with a coach. Alan Seale is a master coach and has established a number of youtube videos to inform others of his coaching practices. You'll find Alan to be warm, unassuming and encouraging – and it's all via the internet, but he will lead you through a discovery process. Why not try another new approach while you are being EPIC and adventuresome? The goal is for you to further tap into another part of yourself that you might be able to use to a larger degree than you have.

The **youtube** video to check out is: Alan Seale – Enlightened Dialogue. Watch and engage with his questions and approach your experiment in a slightly different manner. The video is less than 8 minutes.

**A 90 Day EPIC Experiment:**

---

**In the next 31-60 I want to:**

---

## WEEK SEVEN:

My EPIC experiment is:

Based on my experience with 'Enlightened Dialogue' I plan to:

**Documentation only answers one question this week:** What was your biggest success in relation to your goal? You can stay on the surface with this question, and you can also go a little deeper.

If you walked away from something that you normally would not ignore, this is a success. And, why did you walk away this time? Play with the questions after you identify the success: How was it a success? Why it was different? What shift occurred?

**WEEK 7 DAY 1:** What was your biggest success today in relation to your goal?

NOTE: Play with the following questions after you identify the success: How was it a success? Why it was different? What shift occurred?

**WEEK 7 DAY 2:** What was your biggest success today in relation to your goal?

**WEEK 7 DAY 3:** What was your biggest success today in relation to your goal? How? Why? Shift?

**WEEK 7 - DAY 4:** What was your biggest success today in relation to your goal? How? Why? Shift?




**WEEK 7 DAY 5:** *What was your biggest success today in relation to your goal? How? Why? Shift?*




**NOTE: Play with the following questions after you identify the success: How was it a success? Why it was different? What shift occurred?**

**WEEK 7 DAY 6:** What was your biggest success today in relation to your goal? How? Why? Shift?

**WEEK 7 DAY 7:** What was your biggest success today in relation to your goal? How? Why? Shift?

# WEEK 7 SUMMARY & CELEBRATION!

You might be tempted to skip a celebration because you want to push forward or you are dismissive of what you've done so far. I admire your desire to push forward, but take a moment to give yourself some kudos and celebrate what you've achieved. You only have 5 more weeks to go!

When you look back on this week – what makes you smile?

What was your biggest learning?

# WEEK 8 LAUNCH

**90 Day EPIC Challenge:**

_____

**In days 61- 90 I want to:**

_____

It's time for more experimentation! Let's have fun with a new activity.

**Activity: It would be wonderful if. . .** This is an innocent little exercise that opens possibilities through imagining. Consider your challenge and what magic wand would you like to wave to help you achieve the goal.

For example, if you want to lose weight the 'it would be wonderful if. . .' ideas could be:

- My metabolism would cooperate with me more
- My physical body came into alignment with my desire to look like an athlete
- The cells of my body would cooperate with the mental picture I am holding
- The food burning characteristics of my body kicked into high gear and this process turned into an easy, effortless scenario

This exercise opens possibility since many times we focus on what we don't want but not what we do want. Make a list and review what you've created to determine if there is something that should be added to your plan. Have fun on all aspects and we'll add another dimension at the end of the exercise. You'll never know what is sitting on the fringe of your mind waiting to be discovered.

Wouldn't it be wonderful if:

1.

2.

3.

4.

5.

6.

7.

8.

9.

10.

From your list – highlight the three you are most attracted to and consider how versions of them could show up this week.

**Week 8** is about reverse paranoia. When people are paranoid they believe everything, or many things, are working against them. This week you will hold the belief that the opposite, or the reverse, is occurring and believe that everything is working on your behalf. Regardless of what happens to you this week, believe it is all occurring in alignment with your best interest. Data you collect includes two things:

1. How 'reverse paranoia' impacts you as you respond to the day's events.
2. How your top three from the 'Wouldn't it be wonderful' list show-up for you in a variety of forms.

## WEEK EIGHT:

**My EPIC experiment is:**

**My goal for this week is to:**

**My questions this week are:**

1. How 'reverse paranoia' impacts you as you respond to the day's events.
2. How your top three from the 'Wouldn't it be wonderful' list show-up for you in a variety of forms.

DAY 1:




DAY 2:

## MY QUESTIONS FOR WEEK 8 ARE:

1. How 'reverse paranoia' impacts you as you respond to the day's events.
2. How your top three from the 'Wouldn't it be wonderful' list show-up for you in a variety of forms.

## DAY 3:

## DAY 4:

## MY QUESTIONS FOR WEEK 8 ARE:

1. How 'reverse paranoia' impacts you as you respond to the day's events.
2. How your top three from the 'Wouldn't it be wonderful' list show-up for you in a variety of forms.

## WEEK DAY 5:

## DAY 6:

DAY 7:

WEEK 8 REVERSE PARANOIA - SUMMARY

What surprised me most about this week was:

What I learned about myself this week was:

# WEEK 9 LAUNCH! BRIDGE TO THE FUTURE FIELD OF POSSIBILITY

**90 Day EPIC Experiment:**

---

**In days 60-90 I want to:**

---

You are so close, just 30 days left for more exploration and more discoveries. **Week 9** is about bridging to your dream and how you are pulled toward it. You've been building this muscle each week by crafting your plan, living, experimenting, and thinking about your goal. Now you are going to bridge to it and imagine it even more. This takes a leap of faith but all dreams take this leap because first they are a dream and then they are real. Why should you be different? Oh, I know, you have a lot of answers to that question, but let go of all the reasons why the dream stays a dream and allow all the possibilities to enter.

There's one person you listen to all the time so they are going to join us. Who do we all have in common? You listen to yourself, but frequently you focus on the part of yourself that is trying to keep you safe. Now you need to listen to the future you, the you that achieved this goal. Pause. Let that sink in a little. Somewhere in the field of possibility there exists a place, like a floor of a building, where you achieved this goal. Look off into the distance and you'll see the one that is yours. You might have to tip your head and see a few other things around you, but eventually you will see your place. And once you see yours you won't be able to mistake the feeling, the connection you have with your place. Take a moment to find it in the distance and enjoy the feelings associated with seeing what you have accomplished and all that you have become in the process.

In your mind's eye imagine that your arms are reaching out and connected to your space of accomplishment, and is as strong as anything you have ever experienced. The view is amazing and it's all the things you've ever loved about a place. Coming over the horizon to greet you is your future self – the person you've become in this process and it's funny because you know it's you even from a distance. Yet, you look different and you feel an energy that is different and powerful. The smile that greets you welcomes you and places you at such ease and you realize this is what it means to feel that you are enough and completely accepted, and you feel emotion well up in you. You have so many questions. Sit down and talk to your future self and listen to what has occurred since week 9 of the experiment and even beyond. Have fun with this conversation and start far into the future – 10 or 20 years and then come back to now. Remember this person knows everything about you and accepts you completely, compassionately and with love and understanding that you never even realized could exist. A few conversation starters:

1. How are you?
2. What is our life like now?
3. What is the mantra for our life now?
4. What advice do you have for me in doing this EPIC experiment?
5. How will I know now that I will be successful in the future? (Wow – I can't wait to hear what your future self says!)

Record your insights from the conversation here and onto the next page:

Based on the conversation you had with this special person – shape week 9

1. Create your mantra for the week
2. What was their best advice?

**WEEK NINE LAUNCH:**

**My mantra for this week is**

**My goal for this week is to:**

**My biggest obstacle is and the advice from my future self I will use to overcome it is:**

**DAY 1:** Today reflects the conversation I had with my future self in the following way:

DAY 2: Today reflects the conversation I had with my future self in the following way




DAY 3: Question same as above

**DAY 4:** Today reflects the conversation I had with my future self in the following way

**DAY 5:** Question same as above

**DAY 6:** Today reflects the conversation I had with my future self in the following way

**DAY 7:** Question same as above

# WEEK 9: BRIDGE TO THE FUTURE FIELD OF POSSIBILITY

**Future Self – Summary:** This is a great chapter in my EPIC Experiment because:

**What I learned about myself this week was:**

# WEEK 10 LAUNCH: INSPIRE/LEGACY/INFLUENCE

**90 Day EPIC Experiment:**

**In days 61-90 I want to:**

**How others impact you, and you them.**

There are people who did great things and they inspire you. There are people who could do great things, but they've been stopped short of their goal for reasons beyond their control. They are cheering you on and hand the torch of possibility to you. There are those who won't because they are limited by their own fears and barriers imposed on them by their family, their culture, and countless other things. They need you to show them that dreaming is the first step and experimenting is the second step, and the third step of success NEVER occurs without the first two. Never.

<u>List the people who inspire you.</u> You can identify by name or by groups.

*<u>List the people who were stopped short of their goal but hand you the torch of possibility:</u>*

Note: As I wrote this action journal a wonderful young woman was killed in a shooting accident near her home while walking her dogs. Her husband and family suffered a great loss, and the family who caused the accident is devastated. I push myself to write for her and for her legacy. She was doing great things – running for causes, making a difference, but now she can't. She hands me and others the torch and I push on in her memory so this can be part of her legacy.

*I would like to influence the following people and or groups to dream and experiment!*

Day 1: My behavior today was (inspired, encouraged, or directed toward):
_____

Because of this I was able to:

<u>Day 2: My behavior today was (inspired, encouraged, or directed toward):</u>
_____

<u>Because of this I was able to:</u>

<u>Day 3: (same as above)</u>

*Day 4: My behavior today was (inspired, encouraged, or directed toward):*
_____

*Because of this I was able to:*




*Day 5: (same as above)*

*Day 6: My behavior today was (inspired, encouraged, or directed toward):*

*Because of this I was able to:*

*Day 7: (same as above)*

# WEEK 10: HOW OTHERS IMPACT YOU, AND YOU THEM.

*Summary:* The group that impacted me the most was:

*What I learned about myself this week was:*

# WEEK 11 LAUNCH: QUESTIONS - A DIFFERENCE MAKER

**90 Day EPIC Experiment:**

**In days 61-90 I want to:**

We've talked about how you have ongoing conversations with yourself. I once read that we talk to ourselves in questions, for example: What will I wear today? I wonder what the weather will be? What will I have for lunch? Is my boss in a good mood for our meeting? Have I achieved my EPIC goal for today? Have I exceeded my expectations?

Are you starting to see the trend?

Marshall Goldsmith, an executive coach, further aligned with this idea by focusing with his clients on questions that make a difference – a daily question process. Here's the six he uses that based on his research leads to greater satisfaction. Each question begins with, "Did I do my best to. . ."

Did I do my best to . . .

1. Set clear goals?
2. Make progress toward goal achievement?
3. Be happy?
4. Find meaning?
5. Build positive relationships?
6. Be fully engaged?

He has 32 questions that he asks himself each day. These are questions he crafted to help him shape his behavior and hold himself accountable. He focuses on behaviors he knows are important but are easy to neglect. Then, he pays someone to call him each day to hear his progress. He also has an excel spreadsheet and places a 1 for yes, and 0 for no. Sound familiar? This is what helped shape our initial accountability piece in week 1. Here are a few others he has for himself:

1. How many minutes did you spend writing?
2. How many sit-ups did you do?
3. With how many clients are you current on your follow-up?
4. Did you say or do something nice for your wife? Your son? Your daughter?

As you can see, some have other parameters so you can expand the questions beyond yes or no. You can check out his website for more details: marshallgoldsmith.com.

This week you create your list of questions around the behaviors you want to focus on with your EPIC experiment. Consider the steps you know are important but are not easy to do and list them in your questions. Ideally, have someone call you each day and hold you accountable by asking you the questions. Create a spreadsheet if you'd like and tape it into this journal. You'll have some space for recording your reactions to this process each day, but not a lot of space. Focus your energy on doing the things to get a 'yes' answer to the questions posed each day. Then note how this is helping you, driving you, making you do things, etc. You'll have space for ten questions – but add more to your spreadsheet once you create what you need. Good luck – experiment, challenge yourself, collect data!

Did I do my best to. . .

1.

2.

3.

4.

5.

6.

7.

8.

9.

10.

## TAPE YOUR SPREAD SHEET HERE!

You'll want to include:

- Your questions
- A column for each day to record yes/no
- Use the scoring system to give yourself a 1 for yes, 0 for no.
- Add your columns to determine how your days compare to one another.

**Day 1:** Personal Observations Total Score: _____

**Day 2:** Personal Observations Total Score: _____

**Day 3:** Personal Observations Total Score: _____

**Day 4:** Personal Observations Total Score: _____

**Day 5:** Personal Observations Total Score: _____

**Day 6:** Personal Observations Total Score: _____

**Day 7:** Personal Observations Total Score: _____

# WEEK 11: SUMMARY

What surprised me most about this week was:



What I learned about myself this week was:



**I am amazing because (check all that apply):**
____ I've completed 11 weeks of my EPIC experiment!
____ Tenacity is my middle name!
____ I impress myself sometimes!
____ I really never stop learning about myself!
____ I'm a rock star when it comes to EPIC work!
____ (fill in your own)_____
____ (fill in your own)_____
____ (fill in your own)_____
____ (fill in your own)_____

# WEEK 12 CREATE & LAUNCH

**90 Day EPIC Experiment:**

**In this last week I want to identify my formula for success (read on)**

You completed 11 weeks of your EPIC Experiment. You are tenacity personified. You persevered. You tried different approaches and identified what motivates you, and what doesn't. You succeeded and learned from mistakes. Imagine you were a container that had a lid, and now you've lifted off that lid and discovered there's so much more. In fact now you, the container, are transformed to something else, something more. You occupy a different space, a different plane and you align yourself with those who have a dream and move to achieve it.

Your final week of your 90 Day EPIC Experiment is designed to be a reflection on your experiment. Now is the time to identify <u>your</u> formula for success. You have momentum and you've built the muscle of intention and tenacity. Answer the following questions for finding your current formula for success.

1. In the last 11 weeks the three things that made the biggest impact for me were:
    a. _____
    b. _____
    c. _____
2. My three biggest discoveries about myself were:
    a. _____
    b. _____
    c. _____
3. The three things that influenced me the most in my environment were:
    a. _____
    b. _____
    c. _____

4. My top skills that I used are:
    a. _____
    b. _____
    c. _____
5. My top motivators are:
    a. _____
    b. _____
    c. _____
6. Finish this sentence: I was _____ and now I am _____.
7. Finish this sentence: I thought _____ and now I know _____.

Scenario: Pretend you are meeting a friend for coffee and they have already told you they can't believe how much you've accomplished in the last 11 weeks. They want to know your secret, and vow they will do whatever you tell them to do. How can you tell them all you've learned in 11 weeks? You can't! But, you can share your plan for week 12 and include:

- Your focus for the week
- How you will remain motivated
- How you will record success

This is your plan for the next week. I'll leave you three pages for developing and recording. This is not your final formula. This is your current formula. You will continue to experiment, learn, grow and adapt.

WEEK 12 PAGE 1

WEEK 12 PAGE 2

WEEK 12 PAGE 3

# WEEK 12 CELEBRATIONS!

> *"You don't have to be a fantastic hero to do certain things – to compete. You can be just an ordinary chap, sufficiently motivated to reach challenging goals."* — Edmund Hillary

You did it – you finished 12 weeks devoted to your EPIC experiment. It wasn't easy and maybe you even walked away at one point and then returned. But you are here. Take a deep breath and feel the success of commitment, dedication and progress.

What was the progress you made? Make a note here of the things you accomplished in the past 12 weeks that you are most proud of doing and then we will revisit the EPIC Principles.

# EPIC PRINCIPLES

**Remember the EPIC PRINCIPLES from the beginning? Now is the time to use them as questions to see how your journey impacted you.**

Principle 1: How did your EPIC experiment build a better you?

Principle 2: How did your EPIC experiment tap into potential and possibility in a way you never have before?

Principle 3: How did your EPIC experiment address and remove one or more barriers.

Principle 4: How did your EPIC experiment fill a need for you and for others?

Principle 5: How did your EPIC experiment give you energy?

Principle 6: How did your EPIC experiment inspire you and others through your actions?




Principle 7: How did your EPIC experiment create a new reality?




Principle 8: How did your EPIC experiment challenge you to connect with your true self?




Principle 9: How did your EPIC experiment allow you to learn at a deeper level?




Principle 10: How did your EPIC experiment help you know you are NOT alone? How did others support you either directly or indirectly? How are you part of something much bigger?




Principle 11: (you fill this one in)_____

Principle 12: (you fill this one in)_____

**Last Activity for this EPIC Experiment:** Early on I mentioned this is your story to document and share. Now you've been through 12-weeks and emerged on the other side. At the end of this book I placed my picture and mini biography, but I only did so for you to have as a prototype. This is your book and you are the creator who brought the concepts to life. Have your picture taken holding your completed journal or something that represents your EPIC experiment. When you look into that camera lens do so with a little attitude, embody swagger, think success and then have that picture taken. Place that pic right over mine and then write your mini biography.

This is the little paragraph that says why you were the right one to do this journey, why this was the right time, and why it was important. Of course, you can add anything else you want including the fact that this EPIC experiment is just the beginning (see appendix A for ideas). Type up your biography and place yours over mine. But, before you leave. . .

You need to know we were meant to go down this path together. Thank you for listening to that little voice inside of you that pushed you to do this week after week. We were meant to meet via this action journal and everything you've experienced is building momentum for your future. Share your success and what you've learned – and go light someone else's fire!

# APPENDIX A

*"If you're bored with life — you don't get up every morning with a burning desire to do things — you don't have enough goals."* — Lou Holtz

## LAUNCH FOR YOUR NEXT 90-DAY EPIC EXPERIMENT!

Congratulation on completing your 90-Day EPIC Experiment! You should be pleased with your accomplishment of recording your progress and successes. With the momentum you've created maybe you are going to continue down the path you are on, or maybe you are ready for the next EPIC experiment. If you just need to do some exploring, check out this next activity to get the dreams moving.

This activity is a BIG challenge which allows you to tap into a well of ideas that potentially you haven't dusted off for a while. If you are a task-master, what I am about to propose could drive you crazy, or it could take you to unexplored territory. Because let's confess – you've only just begun. Once you have one success under your belt and a step on **your** success ladder, not someone else's ladder, you will want more. Why? Because you'll realize you have more to give, more to learn, more to experience, and you're having fun! So here it is:

## RECORD 100 GOALS FOR YOUR PERSONAL AND PROFESSIONAL LIFE

Disclaimer: Don't panic! Even if you only record 25, but you do each one – that's awesome!

Proclamation: I am creative, visionary and I dream big! GO!

1.
2.

3.
4.
5.
6.
7.
8.
9.
10.
11.
12.
13.
14.
15.
16.
17.

*Struggling? Put your pen in your other hand! For some reason this allows you to tap into another part of your mind.*

18.
19.
20.
21.
22.
23.
24.
25.

*You're off to a GREAT start!*

26.
27.
28.
29.
30.
31.
32.
33.
34.
35.

36.

37.

38.

39.

40.

41.

42.

43.

44.

45.

46.

47.

48.

49.

50.

*WOW! YOU ARE HALF-WAY THERE! This is a good time to put on some music from a time in your life when you felt invincible! Bring back that swagger...*

51.

52.

53.

54.

55.

56.

57.

58.

59.

60.

61.

62.

63.

64.

65.

66.

67.

68.

69.

70.
71.
72.
73.
74.
75.

GREAT – JUST A FEW MORE! Go BIG and BIZARRE – Why not?!
76.
77.
78.
79.
80.
81.
82.
83.
84.
85.
86.
87.
88.
89.

If you had all the courage you needed, what would you do?
90.
91.
92.
93.
94.
95.
96.
97.
98.
99.
100!

**Congratulations on completing your EPIC experiment list. Now – go have fun!**

"Walk with the dreamers, the believers, the courageous, the cheerful, the planners, the doers, the successful people with their heads in the clouds and their feet on the ground. Let their spirit ignite a fire within you to leave this world better than when you found it." Wilferd A. Peterson, American Author

# APPENDIX B

## GENESIS OF THE 12-WEEK PROJECT

Using journals and goal setting has always been part of my personal journey. Over the years I had journals dedicated to New Year's resolutions, gratitude, daily observations, stream of consciousness, short stories, essays and special projects. I have kept a journal since I was 10 years of age. Each one mentioned I still have. But there is one that was unique.

The book was thin only 100 lined - pages, 6.5' x 9.5' with a green cover which I decorated once I started down the path of my 12-week journey. I had volunteered to diet for 12 weeks using different techniques and approaches and share my experience in a presentation. I chose the slim journal so I could carry it with me and take notes throughout the day. I bought the notebook in Europe when I was on vacation and found it tucked away in my closet. The size was perfect, and I've tried hard to keep this one small for you.

Researching ideas, trying them, obtaining feedback from experts was fascinating and different than my past approaches. All of these were recorded in my green notebook which I eventually decorated with: a picture of Jeff Bridges from an interview I read, a piece from a magazine that said 'Re-Think' and another magazine piece in a small box that said 'YOUR FITTEST YEAR STARTS HERE'. It had an arrow pointing to the inside of the book. I would sit down over lunch with friends on the weekend and pull out my little green book and share my discoveries related to my eating habits, exercise and my progress. They tolerated me, but I didn't care because each new approach had some level of success and another contribution to the presentation. Having to create a presentation was a big factor, because sharing my story forced me to look at the experience from a variety of perspectives – even if they were my own. I had to delve a little deeper, and be open in a different way to overcoming obstacles and to what was working.

The time frame of only 90 days was an ideal time. We are a society of immediate gratification and a New Year's Resolution with a focus of 12 months is daunting. We need to see progress sooner to keep us engaged. I was successful, and the presentation influenced others to do a similar challenge. But, it's the green decorated notebook that remains as a physical testament to my journey. Was it the beginning of this project or was the seed planted with the 10 year old kid who first started a journal? Interesting to contemplate, isn't it?

Mine was a blank book, but I am accustomed to the blank page, others find it frustrating. My goal in the creation of this action journal is to provide direction, some guardrails, but also freedom for you to create and discover during your EPIC experiment.

# APPENDIX C
## RECOMMENDED READING LIST

**The Desire Map: A Guide to Creating Goals with Soul** *by Danielle LaPorte*

**Super Better** *by Jane McGonigal*

**This Year I will. . . how to Finally Change a habit, Keep a Resolution, or Make a Dream Come True** *by M. J. Ryan*

**You Can Heal Your Life** *by Louise L. Hay*

**You are a Badass: How to Stop Doubting Your Greatness and Start Living an Awesome Life** *by Jen Sincero*

**Your Best Year Yet** *by Jinny Ditzler*

(Place your picture over mine – this is your story!)

Sue Hiser is an executive coach, speaker, and facilitator. She's passionate about helping people reach their potential and push beyond their limits. She's a graduate of SUNY Cortland and Kent State University and lives in Columbus Ohio. She's been writing and journaling all her life. *Your EPIC Experience* is her second book and her first action journal.

(Replace my bio with your own and share your story.)